Four Square

Writing in the Content Areas
for Grades 5-9

Writing and Learning Across the Curriculum

Written by Judith S. Gould & Evan Jay Gould

Illustrated by Ron Wheeler

Teaching & Learning Company

1204 Buchanan St., P.O. Box 10
Carthage, IL 62321-0010

This book belongs to

Cover photos by Images and More Photography

Some of the materials on pages 61-112 has been previously published in *the Four Square Writing Method* books by Judith S. Gould and Evan Jay Gould, published by the Teaching & Learning Company.

ISBN No. 1-57310-422-1

Printing No. 98765432

Teaching & Learning Company
1204 Buchanan St., P.O. Box 10
Carthage, IL 62321-0010

Table of Contents

Dear Teacher or Parent,

In classrooms and in homes our students often recite a familiar refrain, "I have nothing to write about!" With language and learning occurring every day there is plenty of writing material available. Integrating writing and content study isn't only about finding something to write. It just makes sense.

Planning and organizing information for writing engages learners in higher levels of thinking and helps your students to move beyond recitation of information to develop deeper understanding.

This book will provide writing ideas and designs for use with all kinds of learning. With these daily activities, special projects and poetry templates, your students can begin to make writing an important tool for comprehension and extension of information across the curriculum. Add the Four Square Writing method, a simple but powerful organizational tool, and your learners will begin to develop connections in their learning.

Sincerely,

Judith Evan

Judith S. & Evan Jay Gould

Section 1:
The Rationale

Simply stated, all learning includes language. The study of science requires reading, discussion and listening to the ideas of others. Musicians and artists enhance their craft through reading about and studying other artists, as well as attending lectures and engaging dialogues with master craftsmen. Even learning mathematics, a system of numerical representations, requires that teachers and learners read about and discuss both method and theory.

It is common practice to employ at least three of the language arts in instruction across content areas.

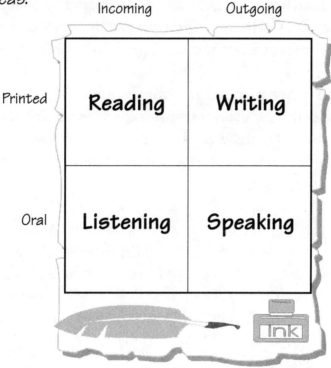

	Incoming	Outgoing
Printed	Reading	Writing
Oral	Listening	Speaking

Even in the most traditional classrooms of content area study, students regularly engage in reading. Textbooks and primary sources are used to enhance instruction. Listening to teachers, instructional media or fellow students provides greater understanding. Speaking in discussion to ask or answer questions is pedagogically advisable in all teaching. Why not, then, make the logical extension and include writing in the study of other subject matter?

In writing, or in preparing to write, students must clarify their thoughts on a topic. They must make sense of what they have read or listened to, and synthesize that information. Writing requires a higher duty of preparation than simply conversing about a subject, because in writing there is an expectation that students include specific content and maintain a logical organization of ideas. With writing, students may use the material learned to draw conclusions, make inferences, or express opinions, rather than simply recite facts.

The addition of writing to content area study can serve to enhance language learning overall because the language arts are interrelated. Thus, practicing writing strategies can help students in reading. Writing can increase the awareness and attention to detail in texts. In preparing ideas for writing, more speaking and conversation can take place. Listening to ideas of others will aid in the preparation of writing.

There are also practical, "real-life" reasons for writing in content areas. So many professions require written reports or correspondence. In the era when e-mail replaces face-to-face exchanges, it is more important than ever that we prepare students to write clearly. Writing is vital to all forms of employability. Whether providing a professional opinion, an estimate for a potential client, or a resume, functioning adults use writing to promote their ideas and opinions.

A prevalence of writing in content areas has appeared on state assessments. Even in the area of mathematics, students are expected to write. Computation and number sense may serve to arrive at an answer, but in many cases, the answer will not earn full score unless it is accompanied by the written rationale detailing the processes used to respond.

In order to prepare our students for these assessments, we need to infuse writing into regular practice in content area study. It will help our students gain deeper understanding of subject matter. Writing across the curriculum will enhance all language learning. Content area writing will help prepare our students for real life writing challenges. But how can writing be included with content area study?

This book seeks to answer that question. In the next section, Everyday Writing Activities, we provide detailed instructions and templates for routine writing activities to be implemented as a part of content area study. These activities have the potential to become routine activities in your classroom. They can function to enhance learning subject matter.

Section 3 features plans and ideas for special writing projects in content area study. These are larger projects. While these may take more time and effort, the production and publication of this type of project will help students to examine a subject in greater detail, while further developing writing skills.

The fourth section of this book provides forms and organizational templates for short poetry writing pieces in the content areas. Whether writing about comparison, definition or procedure, one of these formats may be all your students need to get started.

The final section connects content area learning and the Four Square Writing method. The Four Square, a simple but powerful organizational tool, has been making a difference for writers in countless classrooms. In addition to detail directions about how the Four Square works, we have included templates for the kinds of writing that are typical for many academic assignments.

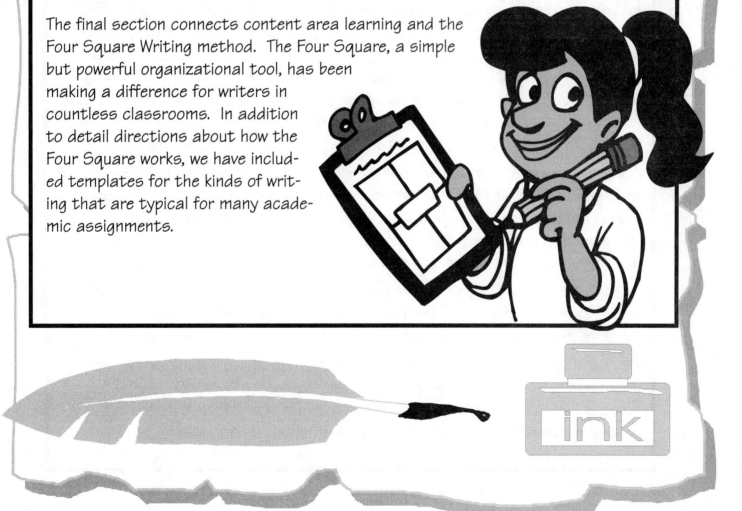

Section 2:
Everyday Writing Activities
Learning Logs

Using a learning log is not unlike maintaining a content area journal. Teachers may use a learning log for students to keep a record of what they have studied, simply by writing from their point of view, what occurred during a particular lesson and what it seemed to mean. Following a lecture, reading selection, discussion or hands-on activity, students would write to reflect on what happened. In writing this way, the students will be dealing with new vocabulary and synthesizing the main concepts of the lesson. A learning log is a place where students would be encouraged to write about the things they did not completely understand. A written record of their questions will be available for subsequent lessons on the material.

A learning log can be maintained as a separate notebook. Many teachers create separate learning logs for content areas in a composition book. Others may choose to require students to maintain a log in their regular notebook alongside any notes from the lesson. It is important to make the log convenient for your situation, so do what is practical for you and your students!

In a typical learning log, students would record the date, subject, "main idea or purpose" of the lesson, and any new vocabulary or content learned. Any questions, misunderstandings or additional inquiries should also be recorded.

By routinely responding to class activities your students will gain experience in writing and analyzing the content material. You need only to set aside a few moments at the end of a class activity for completion of the learning log. This could even be used as an "at-home follow-up" to a classroom activity.

TLC10422 Copyright © Teaching & Learning Company, Carthage, IL 62321-0010

Name _____

My Learning Log Sample

Use the back of the form for a drawing that represents what you learned.

Subject: _____*Math*_____   Date: _____

Main Idea of the Lesson: _*Percentage means the same thing as a part of one hundred.*_

_____

_____

_____

Was this lesson part of a larger unit of study? If so, what unit? _*This is a part of our study of*_
_*decimals.*_____

_____

_____

Describe the learning activity (lecture, pages, project). _*We did some samples out of the math*_
*book on page 142 where we were pretending to buy some clothes that were on sale.*

_____

_____

What new terms or vocabulary were introduced? _*percent, discount*_

_____

_____

_____

Does this lesson remind you of anything else you already know? If so, what? _*This does sound a lot*_
*like when we were doing fractions when things were half because that is like 50*
_*percent.*_____

_____

Record any questions or concepts that you did not understand. _*What I don't get is when*_
*things are a percent off and then another percent off—why we can't just add the*
*two percents and do the multiplication once instead of two times.*

_____

Remember, all your responses should be written in complete sentences.

Name _____

My Learning Log

Use the back of the form for a drawing that represents what you learned.

Subject: _____   Date: _____

Main Idea of the Lesson: _____

_____

_____

_____

Was this lesson part of a larger unit of study? If so, what unit? _____

_____

_____

_____

Describe the learning activity (lecture, pages, project). _____

_____

_____

_____

What new terms or vocabulary were introduced? _____

_____

_____

_____

Does this lesson remind you of anything else you already know? If so, what? _____

_____

_____

_____

Record any questions or concepts that you did not understand. _____

_____

_____

_____

Remember, all your responses should be written in complete sentences.

10

Readers' Responses

Readers' response journals are usually maintained in connection with reading selections about a particular content area of study. While reading, the students are encouraged to jot down revelations, connections or questions concerning the text. This is not meant to be traditional note-taking. It is intended for students to interact with the text. The readers' response entry asks students to synthesize the text and process the information in their own way. The readers' response is often used with fiction texts. In fact, this is a common activity used in literature studies. Asking students to write about what they are thinking while they read can help them to focus on the task. Certainly, any questions or inquiries that arise while reading are appropriate responses to reading.

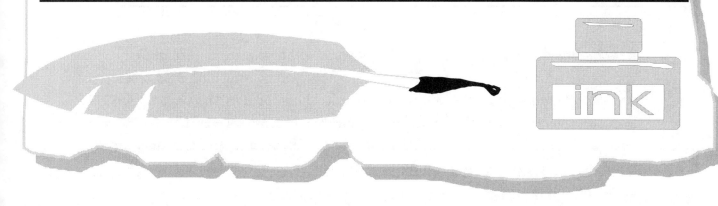

11

Name _____

Readers' Response Sample

Subject: _____ *Social Studies* _____   Date: _____ *November 16* _____

Pages Read: _____ *45-53* _____

Title or Heading of Section Read: _____ *The Era of Isolationism* _____

Page	Response
47	*Isolationism meant that the United States wanted to stay out of the war. Why not? It wasn't our problem. Europe had the problems then.*
49	*Pearl Harbor was a lot like 9/11. It made us pay attention.*
51	*It wasn't a mistake for us to mind our own business. I do the same thing when two kids get into a fight at school. It's not my business.*

Responding to the text means writing down what you are thinking. Do you agree with what you read? Does it remind you of anything else that you know? Would you take the actions that the people in the text took? Do you understand what you are reading? Are there parts of the text that are confusing to you? Write about the things that go through your mind as you read. Ask questions in your response. Perhaps then we can seek the answers.

Name _____

Readers' Response

Subject: _____   Date: _____

Pages Read: _____

Title or Heading of Section Read: _____

Page	Response

Responding to the text means writing down what you are thinking. Do you agree with what you read? Does it remind you of anything else that you know? Would you take the actions that the people in the text took? Do you understand what you are reading? Are there parts of the text that are confusing to you? Write about the things that go through your mind as you read. Ask questions in your response. Perhaps then we can seek the answers.

Double Entry Journals

A double entry journal combines note-taking and response on a single page. In this way, students can make note of important facts and information and also record responses, questions, or connections right along with the material. This may facilitate discussions in class. Students can complete a double entry journal for a variety of classroom activities. For instance, the note-taking column may have student observations and data collected during a science experiment, while the response column has hypotheses and observations. During a film or demonstration, use one column to collect information, and the other column to reflect on the information. You may choose to ask students to take the notes during the class, and then complete the observation and synthesis of information as a follow-up activity. With data and notes at hand, it may prove easier for students to note ideas, mnemonic devices or questions to go along with the material.

Name _____

Double Entry Journal Sample

Subject: _____ *Physical Science* _____   Date: _____ *November 15* _____

Lesson, Demonstration, Lab or Reading: _____ *Science Text* _____

Unit of Study: _____ *Machines* _____

Notes	Response
Simple Machines: Make work easier; no moving parts	Why are they called machines?
Lever: On a resting point—the fulcrum	A hammer is a machine? Fulcrum
Inclined Plane: Flat on one end; used to move things	Skateboard ramp
Wedge: Used to push two things apart; has two sharp points to it.	Teeth? Scissors

Responding to the text means writing down what you are thinking. Do you agree with what you read? Does it remind you of anything else that you know? Would you take the actions that the people in the text took? Do you understand what you are reading? Are there parts of the text that are confusing to you? Write about the things that go through your mind as you read. Ask questions in your response. Perhaps then we can seek the answers.

Name _____

Double Entry Journal

Subject:_____   Date: _____

Lesson, Demonstration, Lab or Reading: _____

Unit of Study: _____

Notes	Response

Responding to the text means writing down what you are thinking. Do you agree with what you read? Does it remind you of anything else that you know? Would you take the actions that the people in the text took? Do you understand what you are reading? Are there parts of the text that are confusing to you? Write about the things that go through your mind as you read. Ask questions in your response. Perhaps then we can seek the answers.

"Don't Get It"s

"Teacher, I don't get it." These words can be very frustrating, especially when you have just completed a prolonged explanation or demonstration of a concept. "I don't get it" provides no information to help to re-teach or clarify ideas for the confused students. If we could only have students focus in on where the loss of understanding occurs, then it might be possible.

It is not uncommon to have students answer questions, in writing, about content material. This may be done after a reading selection or a class activity. In doing so, we hope they will gain a greater understanding of what they have learned, and we can confirm that the lesson "took." But what happens when students don't understand what is covered? Often we receive the blank page, an empty response, or an "I don't get it."

Chances are, the student does "get it," at least part of it. One writing strategy that may help you to help your students is to have them write when they think that they totally don't get it. First, this helps them to focus in on what they do "get." In a math problem, perhaps they did correctly identify the data and the operation to use. The student would write a short description of the attempt made to understand the material, and note the place where things became confusing. This can help us to meaningfully re-teach only the material that the student didn't get.

You may choose to grant partial credit for an explanation and a question even if the final, correct answer was not achieved. In classroom practice, some teachers will not accept an assignment at all if there are blank responses present. The student must at least attempt and document his or her try at understanding. How wonderful it is to provide remediation for exactly what the student is missing!

Name _____

"Don't Get It"'s Sample

Subject: _____ *Math* _____   Date: _____ *October 22* _____

Assignment: _*p. 123, odd numbers*_   Question or Problem No.: _____ *#23*

Unit of Study: _____ *Using variables in algebra* _____

What you know: _They have to pay $350 up front, just to hold the place._ _Then they have to pay $14 for each one of them. That makes it 350 +_ _14(x) = the price. The other way it is just $16 for each of them, so_ _that means 16(x) = the price._

How you tried: _I put in a bunch of different number for the (x) but_ _sometimes it was better one way or the other way._

_____

_____

Where you lost it: _I don't know how many people they have so how can_ _I tell?_

_____

_____

Help me help you. Give it a try. Start with what you know, tell what you did, and let me know where it got lost. With this information, I'll bet we can work together to help you find it!

Name _____

"Don't Get It"s

Subject: _____   Date: _____

Assignment: _____   Question or Problem No.: _____

Unit of Study: _____

What you know: _____

_____

_____

_____

How you tried: _____

_____

_____

_____

Where you lost it: _____

_____

_____

_____

Help me help you. Give it a try. Start with what you know, tell what you
did, and let me know where it got lost. With this information, I'll bet we
can work together to help you find it!

Class Log

A class log is a record of the activities that take place in the class on a particular day. One student may be chosen to maintain the log on a regular basis, or this may be a rotating responsibility in the class. As the log recorder of the day, this student's role is not unlike that of a court stenographer. The idea is to capture as complete a record as possible of the class for that day. The log would include a listing of the major concepts covered, a brief description of the activities done to reinforce those concepts and a notation about the long-term or independent assignments related to these activities. Ideally, a log would be maintained for each day's class so that there is a ready reference of the class activities. During the lesson, the recorder would complete the log page while participating in the learning. At the end of class, the recorder would read aloud the notes made during the lesson. The class can either approve, amend or delete items from the record. In this way, all students would have a part in the collection of this information, requiring that everyone pay attention to the details of the lesson. Upon completion and acceptance of the log entry for the day, the recorder would place the log page in the class book (probably a large three-ring binder). Any handout or supplemental material copies could be placed in the book beside this entry. The log is a tool to help students focus on the details and participate in a summary of the lesson. There is also an added benefit. Absentees need only to look in the log to catch up on the main ideas of the lessons covered that day!

Name _____

Class Log Sample

Subject: _____ *Math* _____   Date: _____ *November 6* _____

Unit of Study: _____ *Fractions* _____

Text pages covered, if any: _____ *159-162* _____

Demonstrations or media viewed, if any: _____

Attachments, if any: _____ *page of homework practice* _____

Class Activities

1. *Mr. B. reviewed homework. Everyone seemed to have a problem with number three.*
   He reviewed it on the overhead.

2. *We broke into groups and did the problem-solving question, #23 on page 160. Mr. B. showed us a lot of*
   different ways to do the answer. Everyone tried #25 alone. Most kids got it. The answer was $3\,{}^{3}/4$ *yards.*

3. *We started on page 161, multiplying fractions.*

4. _____

5. _____

Homework or long-term projects: _____ *page 162, #1-23 odd* _____

Log read? _____ *yes* _____   Additions or corrections? _____ *unit test on Friday, November 10* _____

Recorder signature: _____ *Joe Q. Student* _____

Name _____

Class Log

Subject:_____ Date: _____

 Unit of Study: _____

Text pages covered, if any: _____

Demonstrations or media viewed, if any: _____

Attachments, if any: _____

Class Activities

1. _____
   _____

2. _____
   _____

3. _____
   _____

4. _____
   _____

5. _____
   _____

Homework or long-term projects: _____
_____

Log read? _____ Additions or corrections? _____
_____

Recorder signature: _____

Writing to Activate Prior Knowledge

Many research studies have shown that the best learning happens when we can attach new information to something that we already know. That is why we try to create background information before starting a great lesson. Usually our students have some surface knowledge of what it is that we are studying. The trick to planning and providing lasting learning experiences is to overcome the misconceptions and to then get deeper than the surface!

Although the unit of study has not yet begun, the beginning may be one of the best times to "test" what they know. Students may be able to generate a list of ideas that they think may be related to the topic of study. They may also help you to plan for instructional experiences to overcome misconceptions that they may have about a particular topic. Of course, on the pretest the goal is not to demonstrate mastery of a topic. But having a good understanding of where the students are in their understanding can help to decide where we may go.

The "Prior Knowledge" writing page may be included at the beginning of class notes for the topic of study. Sometimes, after completing this page, you may choose to have students share what they have written. Their responses can be collected in a KWL chart or another fashion to record the starting place for the learning. This tool can be reevaluated at the end of the unit of study. It will serve as a record of the learning that has occurred.

Name _____

Prior Knowledge Sample

What I already know about _____ _volcanoes_ ,

Subject: _____ _Science_ _____   Date: _____ _February 4_ _____

What you know: _Volcanoes erupt. They shoot lava and steam. They are_ _dangerous. They kill people and animals and trees when they hap-_ _pen. Most volcanoes are on mountains. They have a big hole in the_ _top of the mountain so that the lava can get out._

Words you have heard that are related to this topic: _erupt, lava flow,_ _steam, earthquake_

What you think you may learn in this unit of study: _Probably we will learn_ _how volcanoes got there and why they erupt._

This is a survey of what you already know about the subject. It is *not* a test. There are no right or wrong answers. But you will probably be surprised to learn that you know a lot about this topic even before we start studying. Be honest with yourself and really try to think of what you know, or think you know about this topic. This will help us make the learning easier.

TLC10422 Copyright © Teaching & Learning Company, Carthage, IL 62321-0010

Name _____

Prior Knowledge

What I already know about _____.

Subject: _____   Date: _____

What you know: _____

_____

_____

_____

Words you have heard that are related to this topic: _____

_____

_____

_____

What you think you may learn in this unit of study: _____

_____

_____

_____

This is a survey of what you already know about the subject. It is *not a test*. There are no right or wrong answers. But you will probably be surprised to learn that you know a lot about this topic even before we start studying. Be honest with yourself and really try to think of what you know, or think you know about this topic. This will help us make the learning easier.

Student-Generated Questions

In order to ask a meaningful question about a subject, it really requires that one have some insight about the topic. One valuable activity is to have students create "test" questions about the content area of study. Our students should learn the skill of anticipating the questions they may be asked about the material being studied. Building those meta-cognitive skills will help them to become better, more efficient students. A way to encourage this growth is to have students write questions (and answers) that they think may appear on a test of the material.

To facilitate this activity it may be useful to supply students with Bloom's Taxonomy of Thinking Levels' questioning stems. Not only will it inspire question writing, but an awareness of these questions and the level of thinking they require can help our students to gain a better understanding of the way to respond to these questions themselves.

You may actually decide to include some of the students' questions on a teacher-prepared test. This can inspire students to submit well-reasoned questions and answers. In some classrooms, a question submitted by a student that appears on the test will add a bonus of a few points to that student's paper!

Name _____

Blooming Questions

These questions reflect the hierarchy of thinking skills as described in Bloom's Taxonomy[1]. Use these question stems to write questions for discussion, or give them to students to enable them to form their own questions about reading selections. Remember that "Recall" is the lowest level of thinking and "Evaluation" is the highest level according to Bloom.

Recall

- Who? _____
- When? _____
- What? _____
- Describe: _____

Comprehension

- In your own words, restate (retell) _____
- What is the main idea or theme of _____?

Application

- How is _____ an example of _____?
- How is _____ related to _____?
- Why is _____ significant?

Analysis

- What are the features (parts) of _____?
- Why _____?
- Classify _____ according to _____.
- What can you conclude from _____?
- What evidence can you present for _____?
- How does _____ compare with _____?

Synthesis

- What would you predict from _____?
- What ideas can you add to _____?
- What will happen if _____?
- What solutions would you suggest for _____?

Evaluation

- What is your opinion of _____?
- What is the most important _____?
- What criteria would you use to assess _____?

[1]Benjamin S. Bloom, Bertram B. Mesia, and David R. Krathwohl (1964). *Taxonomy of Educational Objectives* (two vols: the Affective Domain & The Cognitive Domain). New York. David McKay.

Section 3:
Special Writing Projects
Brochures

A brochure contains a short, powerful description of the most important statistics on a particular subject. It may also contain illustrations, photographs or graphic representations of the subject. Brochures give a simple but diversified view of a subject. As such, they are a perfect objective for writing projects in content areas.

Brochures come in many varieties. A brochure may be used to invite travel to a particular destination. Brochures advise of special museum exhibits. Brochures can invite us to a performance of theater or symphony. Brochures are offered on items for sale. Brochures are used to advertise seminars and courses. These types of brochures may be created to reinforce and extend content area study.

Imagine a brochure inviting travel to Ancient Greece. It would include descriptions of the most appealing tourist spots. The brochure may invite travelers to visit the dwellings of royalty and to ride through the countryside to see the rustic homes of the peasants. Illustrations or maps would enhance the appeal of the brochure. It is easy to see that the student creating such a brochure will need to engage in a thorough consideration of the topic.

A brochure on a museum exhibit can display any content material. It may feature an exhibit on the study of plate tectonics or the lineage of Chinese empires. The brochure would feature illustrations of one of the featured items in the exhibit. It would tell the viewers what they will learn at the exhibit.

A performance brochure can review a particular work of music, play or other artistic media. A brochure for *Hamlet* may include a synopsis of the plot, as well as information about the playwright. It will entice the audience with illustrations. This brochure may recommend the show to a particular audience, perhaps one that enjoys stories of intrigue and betrayal. Creating a brochure like this requires an in-depth understanding of the material.

A sale brochure will entice us to consider an object of some value. Perhaps students will begin a biology study with a lesson on the function and purpose of the microscope. To gain a better understanding, create a brochure offering it for sale. It may include a diagram of the valuable features of the microscope. The brochure would extol the virtues of the valuable tool to appeal to a potential buyer.

Certainly a course brochure can work for any content area being studied. Advertise the benefits and exciting study of geometrical figures. Include a preview of some of the featured topics of the study. Advertise some of the skills that participants of the class can expect to master upon completion.

The following directions and templates can be used for content area writing projects that are almost without limit! Collect samples of brochures for students to use for samples and ideas. The brochure encourages specific, concise writing and can create a greater understanding of a topic.

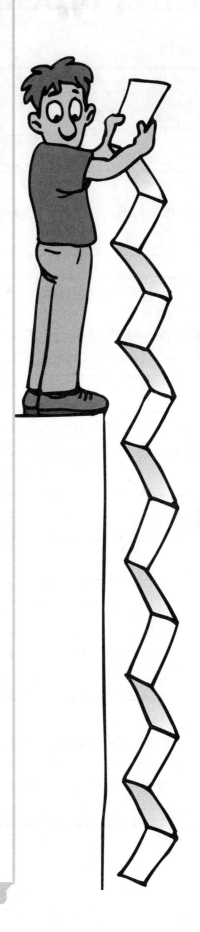

Name _____

Travel Brochure—Information Page

Subject: _____   Unit of Study: _____

Where is it?   _____

_____

What should we expect to see there?   _____

_____

_____

Why would we want to go there?   _____

_____

_____

How would we travel there?   _____

_____

What can we learn or experience by going there?   _____

_____

_____

Are there any souvenir items that may interest visitors?   _____

_____

What special spots should travelers be sure to visit?   _____

_____

_____

Saint Augustine, Florida

The Bridge of Lions

The Nation's Oldest City

Historic St. Augustine, Florida

The nation's oldest city has a host of interesting places to visit. Tour a fort made in the sixteenth century. Imagine the imprisonment of Spanish, French and Native American warriors. Stop by and have a sip from the Fountain of Youth. The nation's oldest schoolhouse still stands. Learn about the earliest European inhabitants of the new land.

Name of place

Picture of the place

A catchy slogan
about the place

Name of the place

Use this area to write a description of the wonderful
time that travelers would have. Be sure to include
specific details and vivid, descriptive language.

Travel Brochure Layout

Name _____

Museum Exhibit—Information Page

Subject: _____   Unit of Study: _____

What are people supposed to learn when they see this? _____

_____

_____

What are some special objects they would see there? _____

_____

_____

What historical people or events may be featured? _____

_____

_____

What questions will this exhibit answer for the viewers? _____

_____

_____

_____

_____

Why is this exhibit more special than others on similar subjects? _____

_____

_____

Are there any souvenir items that may interest visitors? _____

_____

January 21-January 28   10:00 a.m.-6:00 p.m.

The Paterson Elementary Museum
proudly presents
Inside Your Insides

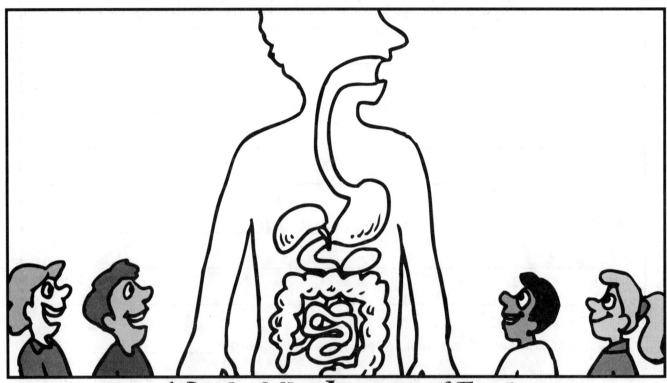

A Look at the Journey of Food

This larger-than-life model of the digestive system is so big that visitors can walk through. Don't worry, umbrellas are supplied during the splash of the digestive juices.

Highlights

• Discover your body's power to break down food.

• Learn how energy is absorbed into the bloodstream.

• Find out how the body disposes of its unwanted food.

Follow the path of your food.

Museum Exhibit Sample

Dates of Exhibit: **Times:**

Title of exhibit

Illustration

What people will learn by visiting   **Highlights/Special Objects**

- List the highpoints here.

- List the highpoints here.

Souvenirs   - List the highpoints here.

Make a catchy slogan.

Museum Exhibit Layout

Name _____

Performance Brochure—
Information Page

Medium: _____   Performer: _____

Artist: _____

What type of performance is this? _____

_____

_____

What would be the highlight for the viewer or listener? _____

_____

_____

Who would most enjoy this performance? _____

_____

_____

Why is this performance different? _____

_____

_____

Tell a little about the composer or playwright. _____

_____

_____

April 17-April 21, 2004   7 p.m.

The Paterson Elementary School

Drama Club Presents

The King and I

This musical theater performance
features over 100 students.
Singing, dancing and fine acting
make the story of this Siamese King
come to life.

Written in the 1950s by Rogers and
Hammerstein, this show was an
instant hit on Broadway.

You will enjoy some familiar tunes:
"Shall We Dance?"; "Getting to Know
You" and "Hello, Young Lovers."

Performance title, date, time, performing group

Picture goes here.

Type of performance

Information about composer

Performance Brochure Layout

Name _____

Item for Sale Brochure—
Information Page

Subject: _____   Unit of Study: _____

Describe the item. _____

_____

_____

_____

Why is this item valuable? _____

_____

_____

Who has owned this article? _____

_____

_____

Who would be interested in an item such as this one? _____

_____

Describe any practical use this item has. _____

_____

_____

Who may have manufactured this item? _____

_____

Thirteen Stars
and Stripes

The Revolutionary Flag

This is a reproduction of the first American flag made by Betsy Ross. She was a widowed upholsterer who lost two husbands during the war.

This represents the birth of a great nation.

Hang it with pride to celebrate our nation.

George Washington, Robert Morris and George Ross asked for the new flag in May 1776. It was officially adopted on June 14, 1777.

Attention
grabber

Name item for sale

Why it is valuable

- List information here.

- Who owned it

Uses of the article

- Who made it

- Cost

Describe item for sale.

Picture

Name _____

Course Brochure—Information Page

Subject: _____   Unit of Study: _____

What is the title of this course? _____

_____

What kinds of things will participants in this course learn? _____

_____

_____

_____

Is there any course that participants should already have taken? _____

_____

Who may be interested in a course like this one? _____

_____

What activities take place in the course? _____

_____

_____

_____

What are the assignments that students complete? _____

_____

_____

What techniques will the instructor use in teaching? _____

_____

_____

Concert Chorus

Meets: Monday and Wednesday 2:30-3:30

Place: The Auditorium

All About Concert Chorus

- You will learn to read music.
- Make friends while learning.
- You will learn how to sing your best.
- Perform for your teachers and friends.
- Listen and learn from the director.
- If you like music, this is for you!

Course Brochure Sample

Title of course

Times: **Place:**

Illustration

All About the Course

- Courses that should come before this one

- Activities and assignments

- The way the teacher teaches this

Course Brochure Layout

The "How-To" Guide

The "how-to" guide provides readers a succinct and specific explanation about how to perform a certain operation. It is usually written in numbered or lettered steps. These actions, when taken in sequence, will help the reader to succeed with the procedure. Often the how-to guide contains illustrations and diagrams to make the directions more accessible for the reader.

It used to be that how-to applications were almost exclusively for the benefit of assembling items. With the advent of self-help and the "For Dummies" series of books, there are how-to guides available for everything from the internet to meditation.

Imagine a science student composing a "How to read the Periodic Table of Elements" guide. This certainly requires that they, themselves, have a great understanding of the topic. A math student's completion of a "How to Solve a Quadratic Equation" requires they know this information so well that they can explain it to others.

Putting the steps to such operations into words and illustrations requires that students make a deeper evaluation of the material which leads to greater understanding.

Name _____

"How-To" Guide—Information Page

Subject: _____   Unit of Study: _____

What are we instructing readers to do? Why would they want to do this?

_____

_____

_____

What materials will the reader need in order to do this job? _____

_____

_____

List the steps, by number or letter. Be sure to use clear, specific language.

_____

_____

_____

_____

Include illustrations with your directions. What will you illustrate? _____

_____

_____

How to Grow a Bean Plant

Materials
soil
water
cup
a dried bean seed
a sunny spot

1. Fill your cup with soil. Leave room at the top.

2. Press your seed down into the center, about $1^1/2$ inches.

3. Pat the soil across the top.

4. Place in a sunny spot and keep soil moist.

5. In 7-10 days you should see a sprout!

Picture of the completed work

How to _____

Materials that are needed for this project

Step-by-step information. Number each step.

"How-To" Guide Layout

Section 4:
Poetry Forms for Content Writing
The Definition Poem

In nearly every content area of study students learn new terminology and definitions. The names of people, places and things fill our history books. Applying the learning of content material to this writing form can make acquisition of these facts fun!

For the definition poem the writer uses as many different perspectives as possible to define an item or event. For instance, the squirrel and the logger have different reasons to dislike the wildfire, so they may define it differently based on perspective. This form puts all the perspectives in sequence.

Wildfire
A threat to new neighborhoods
A nightmare to insurance companies
A livelihood for the brave fire fighter
A case for Federal Disaster Areas
High alert to small mammals
A target for a small plane's watery payload
A more and more common news story
The source of debate between naturalists and
　　loggers
Consumer of dead underbrush
A source of renewal to the forest at large
Liberation and rebirth for tired, old giants
The origin of brown air, that sticks in the back
　　of your throat

Definition Poem Planning Page

What is your topic? _____

Start out with a dictionary definition, or the definition from the glossary of your textbook.

_____

_____

Which people, things or animals would be interested in this topic? Why would they be interested?

Who	Why

Now decide which ones you would like to include. Decide what order you would like to have for your ideas. Find a "snappy" one for the ending. Define the item the dictionary way, and then let each person, thing or animal have its chance to define the item, too.

The Diamante

This poem is about contrasts. It takes two opposing ideas. The first half of the form is for describing Item one as follows:

Line 1:	Name item 1	Earth's moon
Line 2:	Two adjectives describing item 1	Solid, cratered
Line 3:	Three "ing" or "ed" words describing item 1	Rotating, spinning, pulling
Line 4:	Two nouns or names for item 1 and two nouns or names for item 2	Lunar, nighttime, solar, daytime
Line 5:	Three "ing" or "ed" words describing item 2	Shining, heating, burning
Line 6:	Two adjectives describing item	Gaseous, bright
Line 7:	Name item 2	Our sun

Diamante Planning Page

What two things will you be writing about?

Item 1: _____

Item 2: _____

For each item, think of two adjectives (describing words).

Item 1: _____

Item 2: _____

Now think of three verbs (action words) that end in "ing" or "ed" for each item.

Item 1: _____

Item 2: _____

For each item, think of two nouns or names of people, places or things.

Item 1: _____

Item 2: _____

Now it's time to arrange your diamante.

Line 1:   Name item 1 _____

Line 2:   Two adjectives describing item 1 _____

Line 3:   Three "ing" or "ed" words describing item 1_____

Line 4:   Two nouns or names for item 1 _____

Line 4 (cont'd.): Two nouns or names for item 2 _____

Line 5:   Three "ing" or "ed" words describing item 2 _____

Line 6:   Two adjectives describing item _____

Line 7:   Name item 2 _____

The Noun Poem

This form asks students to describe a place or a setting based on a list of the people, places and things that one would see there. The nouns (which may be described with adjectives, of course are listed. Together they can create an image of the setting or time.

Colonial America
Horse-drawn carriages
Ladies in corseted gowns
Men wearing powdered wigs
Vast farmlands
British officers
Lofty trade ships
Important governors
Hard-working citizens
Friendly Indians
A rising spirit of revolution

Name _____

Noun Poem Planning Page

What place or event will you be writing about?

_____

_____

Look at a picture of the place or the event as it happened. If you cannot see a picture, think of all you have read and learned about this place or event. If you were standing there, what would you see? How would it look? Use this chart for the things you see and some describing words to go with each.

What I See	Describing Words

Now decide which ones you would like to include. Decide what order you would like to have for your ideas. Find a "snappy" one for the ending.

Inside Out Writing

This is another way to describe something. When we start at the deep, inner core of our topic we have to really understand it well. It may be useful to have the textbook or reference material available for this one.

Plant Cell

The Nucleolus, where RNA is stored

The Nucleus, the brains of the operation

A Nucleus wall to protect the powerful

A sea of cytoplasm

Golgi body Mailboxes Etcetera at the cellular level

Endoplasmic Reticulum Smooth and Rough Interstate highways and local
   roads

The Vacuole, shapely space-keeper

Mitochondrion, the generator that powers the cell

Cell Membrane, border patrol with selective security screening

Cell Wall, an armed guard with a strong network in its profession

Name _____

Inside Out Poem Planning Page

What is your topic? _____

Start out with a dictionary definition, or the definition from the glossary of your textbook.

_____

_____

If you were to start in the exact center of this object, and then take a journey to the outside, what would you see along the way? How would you describe each thing you see? Use the chart to make your notes.

What I See	Description

Now decide which ones you would like to include. Make a "snappy" one for the ending.

The Cinquain

A cinquain is a five-line poem (the French word for *five* is *cinq*) that defines a person, place or thing. This is a form that is accessible and enjoyable for learners of all ages and ability levels. It works well with content area learning.

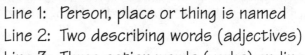

Line 1: Person, place or thing is named
Line 2: Two describing words (adjectives)
Line 3: Three action words (verbs) ending in "ing" or "ed"
Line 4: A two- or three-word phrase that tells about the topic
Line 5: The topic again. May be the same as line 1, or another way of stating it.

Abraham Lincoln	Volcano
Honest, tall	Big, powerful
Speaking, thinking, guiding	Rumbling, erupting, exploding
On the penny	Mt. St. Helens
President	Volcano

Cinquain Planning Page

Name your topic.

_____

Think of two adjectives (describing words).

1: _____

2: _____

Now think of three verbs (action words) that end in "ing" or "ed."

1: _____

2: _____

3: _____

Think of a two- or three-word phrase about your topic.

_____

For the ending, state the topic again, or say it a different way.

Line 1:   Person, place or thing is named _____

Line 2:   Two describing words (adjectives) _____

Line 3:   Three action words (verbs) _____

Line 4:   A two- or three-word phrase _____

Line 5:   The topic again _____

Acrostic Poetry

This is likely the most accessible and flexible poetry form. It can be done with a word or a phrase. Simply line up the topic along the margin of the paper. Write it vertically down the edge. Then use each letter as the first of the word that will begin the line of poetry.

Can you imagine the world without those machines?
One can be found almost everywhere.
Mailmen, teachers, and airport workers
Put information in
Using them can be so fast and easy
Try one and you'll see
Everyone is using them
Ready for the new millennium

Or this can be done using a phrase:

We are the people of the United States of America
The greatest nation in the world
People united to meet our great goals together

Biographical Poem

Try this poem form using an historical figure. This is the form of the poem. You may use as many or as few of these as possible.

First name
Mother/Father/Daughter/Son/Sister/Brother/Aunt (etc.) of
_____
Who loves _____
Who fears _____
Who wishes for _____
Who would like to _____
Who would never _____
Who dreams of _____
Who would like to create _____
Who needs _____
Who would like to see _____
Who wants _____
Who wants to be remembered as _____
Last name

Dr. Martin Luther
Husband of Coretta Scott
Who loved family and mankind
Who feared nothing
Who wished for equal standing
Who would have liked to live to have seen the day his dream came true
Who needed the help of all people
Who wanted the nation to embrace true freedom
Who would want to be remembered as a man of his people
King, Jr.

Using the Four Square Writing Method for Content Area Writing

The Four Square is a simple, open-ended graphic organizer that was designed to help students focus, organize and support their writing with detail. While simple in its design, it is very open-ended in its application.

Overview of the Four Square

Reason or Example

- Supporting detail

- Supporting detail

- Supporting detail

Reason or Example

- Supporting detail

- Supporting detail

- Supporting detail

Topic Statement:

_____

_____

_____

_____

Reason or Example

- Supporting detail

- Supporting detail

- Supporting detail

Wrap-Up Sentence

One sentence that concludes the writing, which includes the topic statement, along with the three reasons or details.

Pre 4□ Activities
Understanding Relationships

In order to organize writing into topics and sub-topics, we first need to explore the ways things are related. Some words, objects or ideas are broad and can encompass other ideas. Beneath these broad words, objects or ideas we can give examples, definitions or sub-categories. Before students can develop the main idea and supporting detail, they must understand that the subordination of one idea to another is natural and something they have observed in their world.

Provide multiple examples of this relationship's practice. Students can be challenged to think of as many subtopics to an idea as possible, using cereal brands, rock bands, football, baseball, soccer or hockey teams, television programs or any other familiar and comfortable topic. We want students to feel like this is a "game" and to achieve immediate success in writing instruction.

Reproducible worksheets are provided on pages 64 and 65 for practicing this important concept.

Understanding Relationships

Directions: Fill in the lines beneath the topic with three items that belong as subtopics.

People

Subjects

_____

_____

_____

_____

_____

_____

Things to Drink

Birds

_____

_____

_____

_____

_____

_____

Name _____

Understanding Relationships

Directions: Fill in the lines beneath the topic with three items that belong as subtopics.

Animals

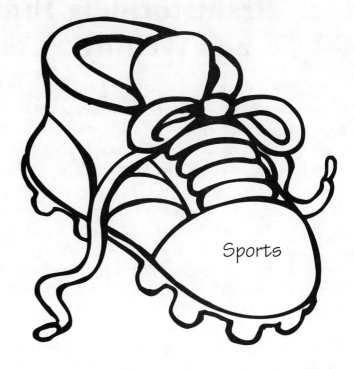

Sports

_____
_____
_____

_____
_____
_____

Fruit

Food

_____
_____
_____

_____
_____
_____

Step 1

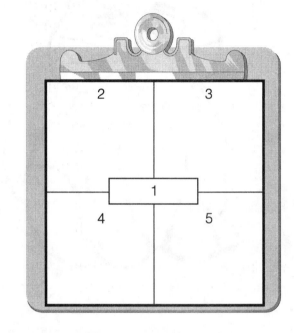

Brainstorming Three Supporting Ideas and Writing a Concluding Sentence

In this step we move our brainstorming activity onto the four square format. We will continue our practice in understanding the relationships between ideas. The main, broad or general idea is placed in the center box of the four square (box 1). Boxes 2, 3 and 4 are used for supporting detail. The remaining box, lower right (box 5), will be employed to build a summary or concluding sentence. In practice, this is referred to as the "wrap-up" sentence because it encompasses all the ideas developed in the four square in the form of a series sentence.

While introducing the series sentence on instruction this early may cause technical difficulties, the importance of the wrap-up sentence cannot be understated. This all-encompassing sentence is the basis for future development of introductory and concluding paragraphs. Indeed, the wrap-up is truly the statement of the three-pronged-thesis-and-development paper. So just remind students of the need for commas in the serial sentence and get beyond the technical. **Throughout four square instruction, spelling and most technical matters are deemphasized.** Our goal is to GET STUDENTS TO THINK!

WRAP UP!

The introduction of the "wrap-up" sentence this early in organization practice serves well to prepare students for writing their statements of thesis. This wrap-up sentence will encompass all the main ideas of the paper and include the topic. Certainly the students needn't worry about developing a thesis at this point, but the foundations have been built.

The brainstorming should be an engaging challenge to students, encouraging even reluctant writers to participate!

It is recommended that students practice this very basic four square repeatedly. Whole class modeling and cooperative writing can be used. Small group work is also very effective in these early stages of instruction on the organizer. The basic four square provided on page 68 can be duplicated on a transparency for an overhead projector or opaque machine. Each group then draws a topic "out of a bag" and the group recorder writes it in the center box of the transparency with a wet-erase pen. The group then completes the four square cooperatively. The use of groups removes any intimidation and also promotes the idea that the four square is a friendly, game-like approach to writing. Teams may even race one another. Also, students enjoy writing on the transparencies and placing them on the machine!

At this stage, students will be happy to be reminded that thus far you have asked them to write only one sentence!

(Reproducible workbook practice pages for this stage follow the transparency reproducible on pages 69 and 70.)

Pretzels	Popcorn
Snacks	
Peanuts	Pretzels, popcorn and peanuts are snacks.

This example of a basic four square shows the relationships between the main idea–"snacks"–and the three sub-ideas–"pretzels, popcorn and peanuts."

Group: _____

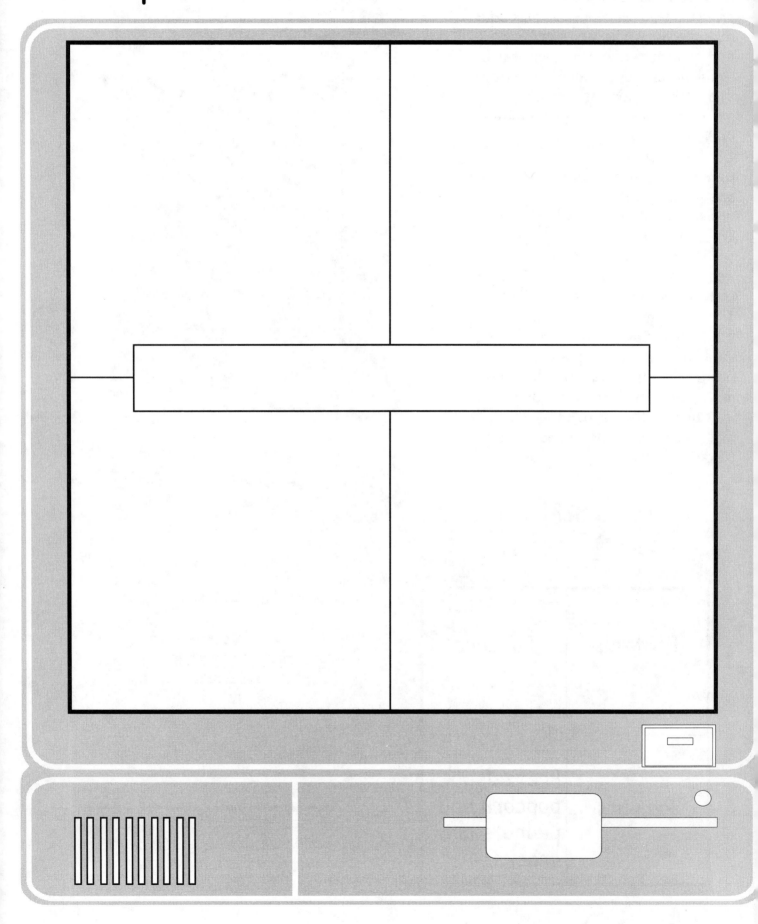

Name _____

Directions: Complete the four square with one item in each box and a wrap-up sentence.

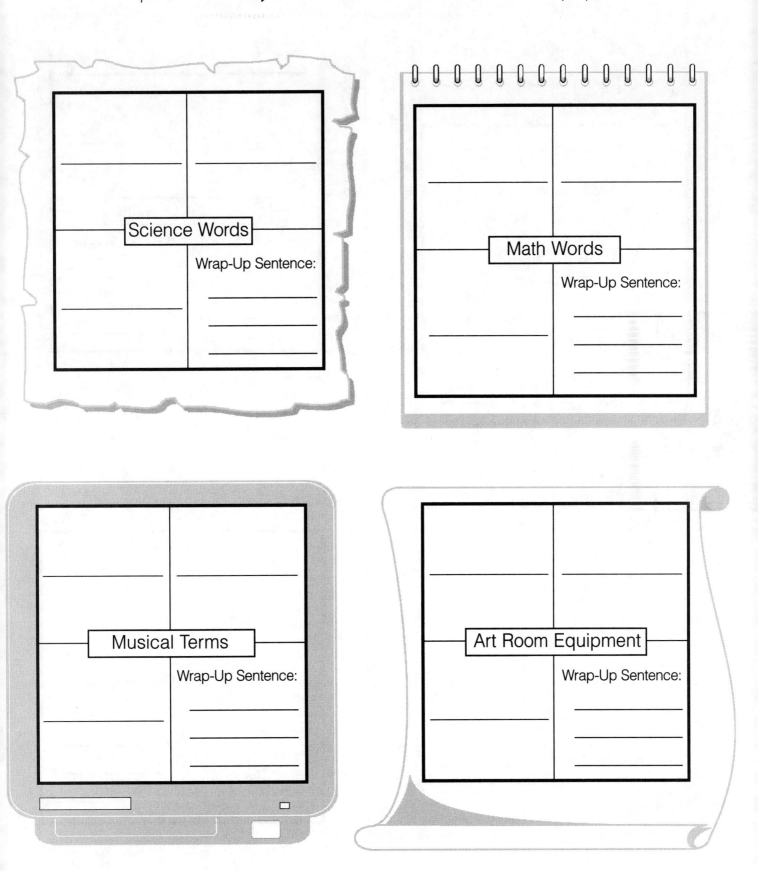

Science Words

Wrap-Up Sentence:

Math Words

Wrap-Up Sentence:

Musical Terms

Wrap-Up Sentence:

Art Room Equipment

Wrap-Up Sentence:

Name _____

Directions: Complete the four square with one item in each box and a wrap-up sentence.

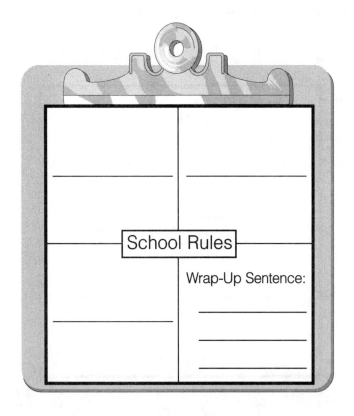

School Rules

Wrap-Up Sentence:

_____
_____
_____

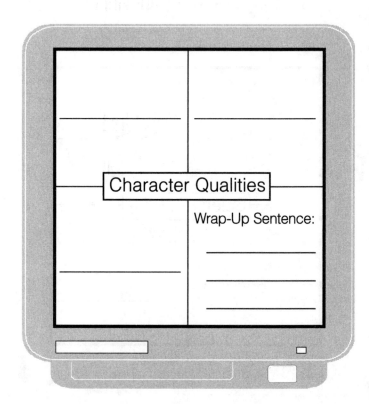

Character Qualities

Wrap-Up Sentence:

_____
_____

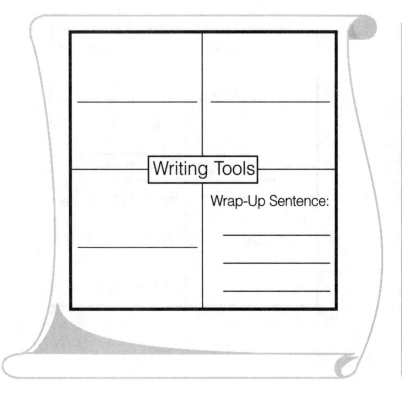

Writing Tools

Wrap-Up Sentence:

_____
_____
_____

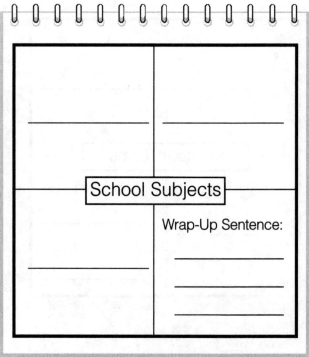

School Subjects

Wrap-Up Sentence:

_____
_____
_____

TLC10422 Copyright © Teaching & Learning Company, Carthage, IL 62321-0010

Three Supporting Ideas and a Concluding Sentence Using an Expository or Persuasive-Type Prompt

Now the stage has been set for developing real logical reasoning and persuasion. The next part of Step 1 involves only a small change in the challenge. The center box will now contain a complete sentence (prompt). In previous exercises there was only a word or short phrase for the topic. The introduction of a complete sentence now alters the requirements of boxes 2, 3 and 4. These boxes must now contain **reasons, examples or explanations** that prove box 1 true. These reasons, examples or explanations must all be different from one another and must be real, quantifiable reasons, not merely matters of opinion.

Students may not easily identify the distinction between fact and opinion. If they believe that "fun," "cool" and "awesome" are quantifiable reasons and different from one another, they will have difficulty building a good persuasive or expository piece of writing. To help them understand that individual perceptions are very different and that an opinion is not reliable, start by telling two stories.

Story 1

Teacher: I have just heard a great song. It is cool, awesome and great. Do you want to hear it?

Students: (*shouting*) Yeah!

Teacher: Great. I didn't know you were into opera!

Point out that opera is cool, awesome and great to you, but you may not wish to endure any music that is cool, awesome and great to them.

Story 2

Teacher: I've got a great new food here. It's delicious, wonderful and so tasty.

Students: (*if they fall for it a second time*) Yeah!

Teacher: Great. I didn't know you kids liked liver.

For further practice in developing strong or persuasive reasons and examples, encourage students to "prove" the prompting sentence. The ubiquitous courtroom drama on television has exposed kids to a great deal of persuasive argument. This can help them relate to the need for quantifiable reasons.

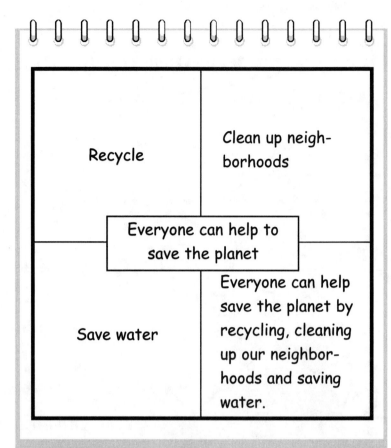

Recycle	Clean up neighborhoods
Everyone can help to save the planet	
Save water	Everyone can help save the planet by recycling, cleaning up our neighborhoods and saving water.

To provide continuity from now on, it is recommended that you use the same prompt for introduction of additional stages. The familiarity and predictability of the topic will provide comfort for students while learning additional steps.

The "save the planet" example will be used for introduction of future stages of the four square development.

One area of difficulty that you may encounter at this stage involves the introduction of a conjunction in the wrap-up sentence. *Since, because* or *due to* usually work nicely in this situation.

Because the wrap-up is now stringing together different ideas and objects, there is no need to give some attention to the flow of writing in the serial wrap-up sentence.

With modeling and ample group practice (overhead transparency or opaque for sharing), students quickly assimilate the language needed for a nicely flowing wrap-up sentence.

If a student is writing wrap-up sentences without consideration of the flow in the series of ideas, it can be read aloud in a straight monosyllabic monotone deemed the "Tarzan" voice. They quickly understand that the sentence lacks flow when it is spoken in "jungle talk." They will seek to avoid a "Tarzan" sentence when they hear it read aloud.

Name _____

Directions: Write a reason, example or explanation in each box to support the main idea sentence in the center box and write a wrap-up sentence.

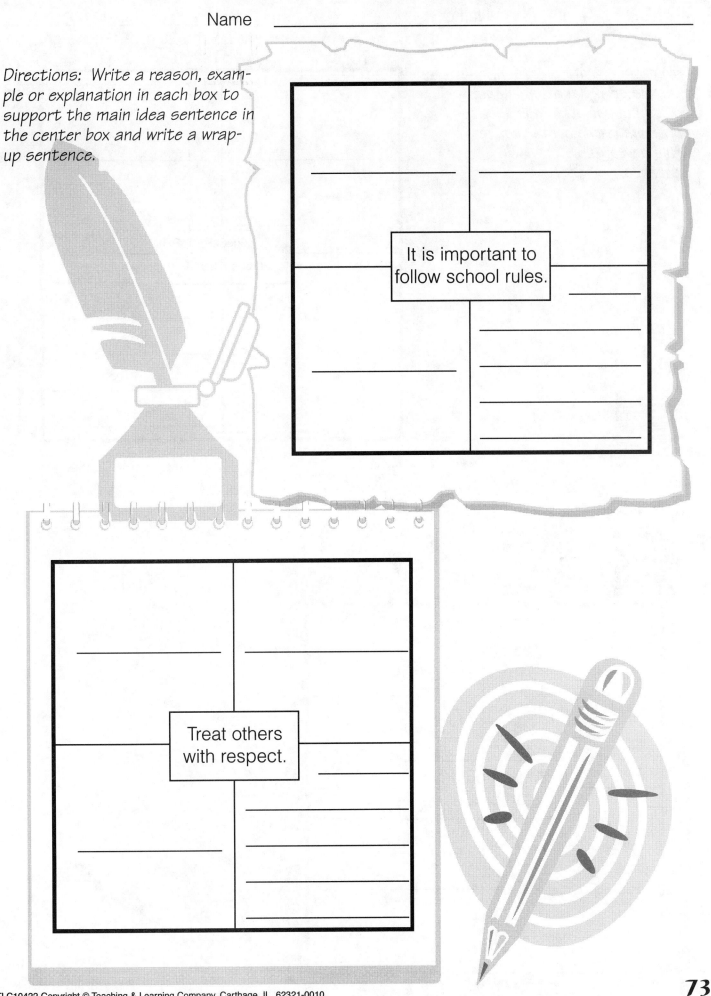

It is important to follow school rules.

Treat others with respect.

Name _____

Directions: Write a reason, example or explanation in each box to support the main idea sentence in the center box and write a wrap-up sentence.

Volcanoes can be violent.

Kids should not start smoking.

Step 2

4☐ + 3

Adding Supporting Details

The reasons, examples or explanations cre-ated in the four square stage of organization now need further development. In a sense, boxes 2, 3 and 4 will now be "four squared" independently. These details will be developed later to make up the meat of the paragraphs in the body of the composition. Using the four square to develop these ideas ensures that details are aligned with main ideas, and a topic sentence starts every paragraph.

Students may not be so easily convinced of this need for expansion of their thoughts. One way to point out the need for elaboration is to "read" the story created by four square alone.

Recycle	Clean up neigh-borhoods
Everyone can help to save the planet.	
Save water	Everyone can help save the planet by recycling, cleaning up our neighborhoods and saving water.

Adding detail and support poses difficulty for some students. Many are not accustomed to elaborating. Writing is not like a multiple-choice examination, and starting their brains may be painful for some kids!

RECYCLE BIN

The story created by our example would read as follows:

> Everyone can help to save the planet. If we all recycle there will be much less trash around. Everyone can help clean up his or her own neighborhood. Save some water to help Earth. Everyone can help save the planet by recycling, cleaning up our neigh-borhoods and saving water.

If read orally, the students will identify the repetition and need for detail to enhance the story.

Occasionally students will need some prompting to elaborate on their subject. For an item in boxes 2, 3 and 4, ask students to prove, clarify or give examples of the word or phrase at the top of the box. "What's so good about it?" or "What's great about this reason/example?" often engages the students' imaginations a bit.

It is important to remind students that *there may not be a repetition* anywhere on the four square.

Recycle • newspapers • glass • plastic containers and bottles	Clean up neighbor-hoods • pick up trash • use a wastebasket • never litter
Everyone can help to save the planet.	
Save water • on the lawn • when brushing teeth • showers not baths	Everyone can help save the planet by recycling, cleaning up our neighborhoods, and saving water.

Although you have not yet asked students to take their writing off the organizer and into paragraph form, it is valuable to read them the essay in its formation. At this stage this is the essay.

Everyone can help to save the planet.

If we all recycle there will be much less trash around. Newspapers can be recycled. Glass is as good as new when it is recycled. When plastic is recycled it is cleaned up and used again.

Everyone can help clean up his or her own neighborhood. If you see trash, pick it up. Use a wastebasket. Make sure that you never litter.

Save some water to help Earth. Don't use so much water on the lawn. Shut the faucet off when you brush your teeth. Showers use less than baths, so why not switch?

Everyone can help save the planet by recycling, cleaning up our neighbor-hoods and saving water.

Because of difficulty that some students encounter during this step of instruction (elaboration), it is recommended that there be ample opportunity for practice. The lessons work well in modeling, group work and individual drills. The overhead transparency group project is terrific at this stage, and each group can have a recorder and a reporter who will read the "story" during sharing.

At this stage you can preview to students that they have done all the hard work of writing a five-paragraph essay!

Name _____

Directions: Write a reason, example or explanation in each box to support the main idea sentence in the center box. Then give three details for each and write a wrap-up sentence.

- _____
- _____
- _____

- _____
- _____
- _____

| It is important to follow school rules. |

- _____
- _____
- _____

_____
_____
_____

- _____
- _____
- _____

- _____
- _____
- _____

| The oceans are worth protecting. |

- _____
- _____
- _____

_____
_____
_____

Name _____

Directions: Write a reason, example or explanation in each box to support the main idea sentence in the center box. Then give three details for each and write a wrap-up sentence.

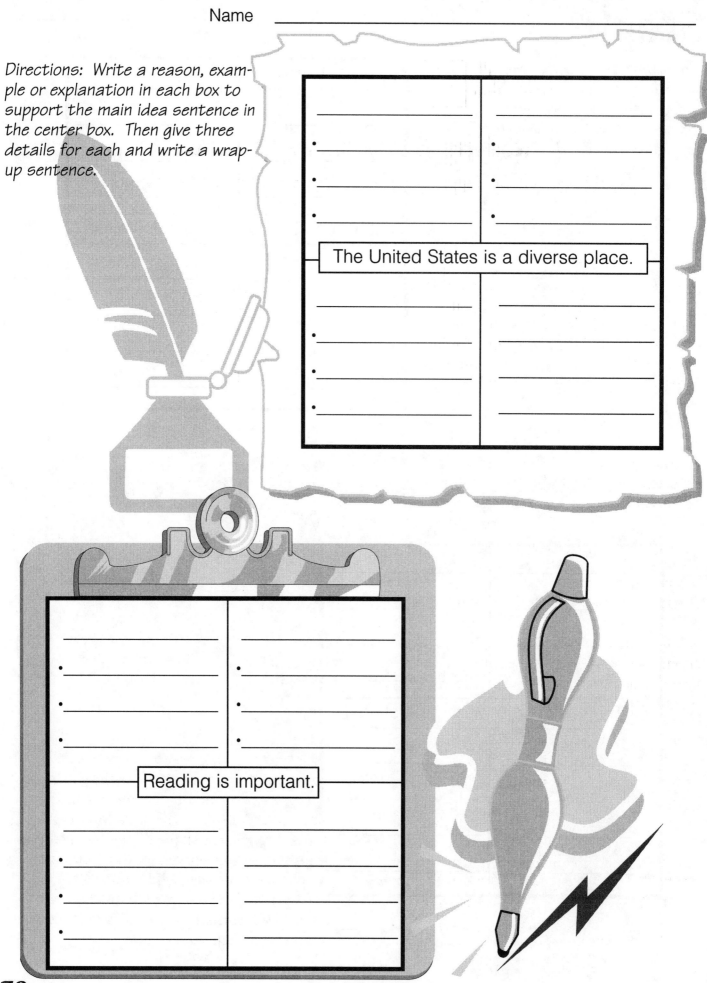

_____
• _____
• _____
• _____

_____
• _____
• _____

| The United States is a diverse place. |

_____
• _____
• _____
• _____

_____
_____

_____
• _____
• _____
• _____

_____
• _____
• _____

| Reading is important. |

_____
• _____

_____
• _____

Step 3

4□ + 3 + C

Adding Connecting Words to Provide Transition Between Thoughts

By now students are developing their thesis (box 1) into three reasons, examples or explanations (boxes 2, 3 and 4) and supporting elaboration. Because the three reasons, examples or explanations are different from one another, the essay is in need of a connection of these differing ideas to provide flow and readability.

Transition words, or as the formula calls them CONNECTING words, can bridge the gap between ideas. If there are two similar ideas, there is an appropriate connecting word to link them. If there are contrasting ideas, there are words that key us to the difference. These connecting words also provide smooth reading when changing paragraphs. Use of these words is critical to successful writing. In fact, it is so critical that students should not be asked to remember them. Color-code connecting words on wall posters, and make them available whenever students write. (See pages 81-84.)

To introduce the concept of connecting words to students, ask for a show of hands of those who have ever worked a puzzle. Most students can identify a puzzle piece and are familiar with its design. Explain that connecting words are the "little sticking out part" of the puzzle piece; they are words that do the same job as that part. Connecting words hold the different pieces of an essay together.

This explanation lends itself well to the presentation of the connecting word wall posters. To ensure success, the words are color coded. Because box 1 is the beginning of the piece, no connection is necessary. Box 2 is coded green (*green* means "go"). Boxes 3 and 4 are yellow to signify moving along cautiously. Box 5 is red, for we are preparing to stop.

Students love choosing connecting words. They absolutely cannot get this stage "wrong" as long as they select the word from the appropriate list. This fosters confidence in students, and this "easy" stage is a break from the more intense brain work required in "+3."

Again provide ample practice with this new step of instruction in modeling, group and individual settings.

The following pages are wall posters and workbook pages for this step.

To begin with Recycle • newspapers • glass • plastic containers and bottles	Also Clean up neighborhoods • pick up trash • use a wastebasket • never litter
Everyone can help to save the planet.	
Additionally Save water • on the lawn • when brushing teeth • showers not baths	In conclusion Everyone can help save the planet by recycling, cleaning up our neighborhoods, and saving water.

Continue to read aloud all examples as they are completed. This will facilitate the change over to composition.

The oral reading of our essay at this stage (Remember, students are writing *only in four square form.*):

Everyone can help to save the planet.

If we all recycle there will be much less trash around. Newspapers can be recycled. Glass is as good as new when it is recycled. When plastic is recycled it is cleaned up and used again.

Everyone can help clean up his or her own neighborhood. If you see trash, pick it up. Use a wastebasket. Make sure that you never litter.

Save some water to help Earth. Don't use so much water on the lawn. Shut the faucet off when you brush your teeth. Showers use less than baths, so why not switch?

Everyone can help save the planet by recycling, cleaning up our neighborhoods and saving water.

Wall Poster

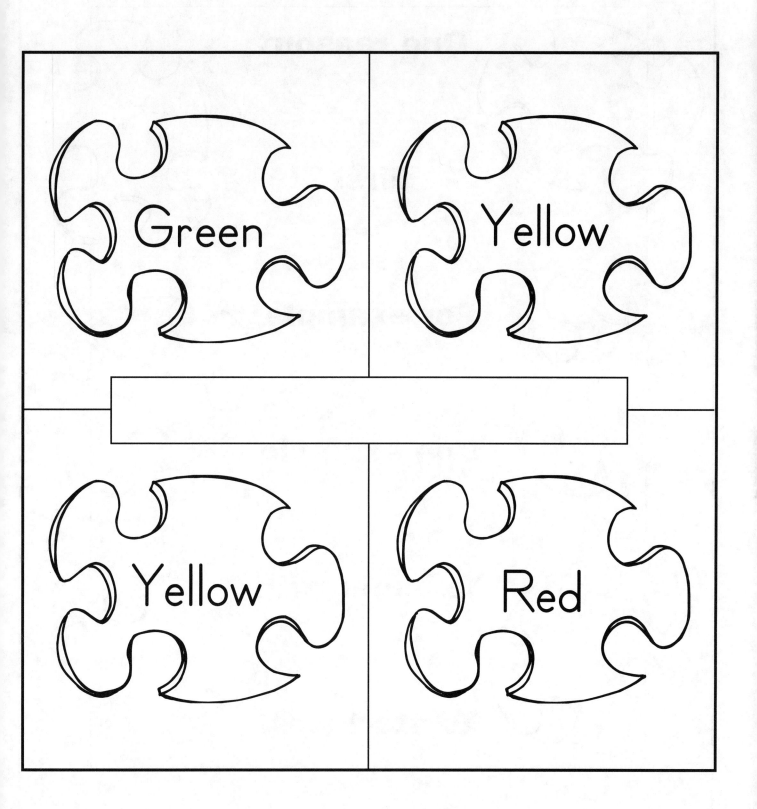

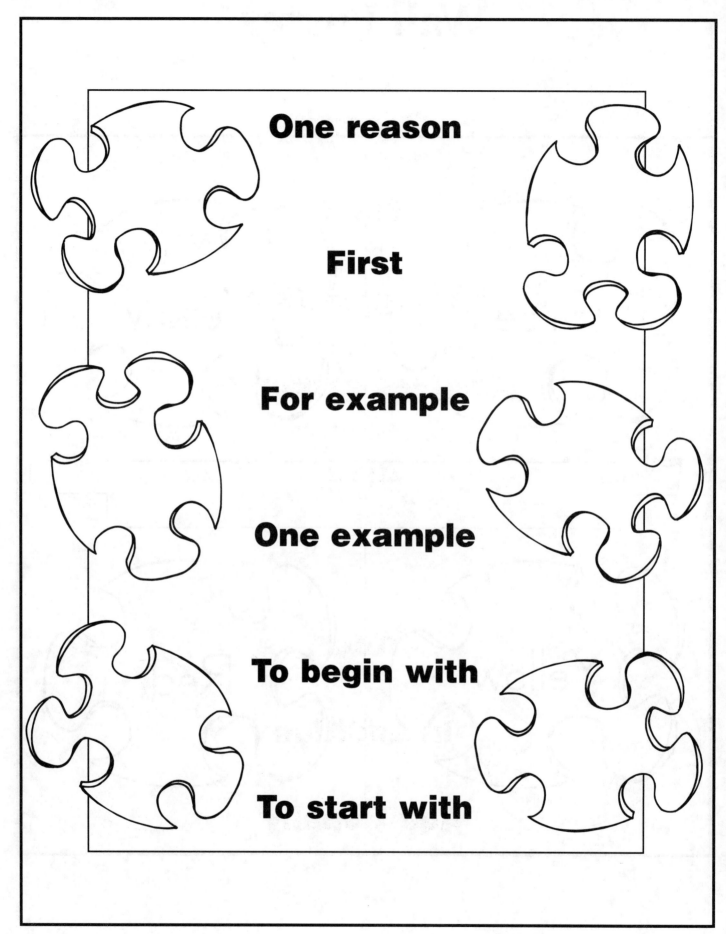

One reason

First

For example

One example

To begin with

To start with

Color the border of this poster green.

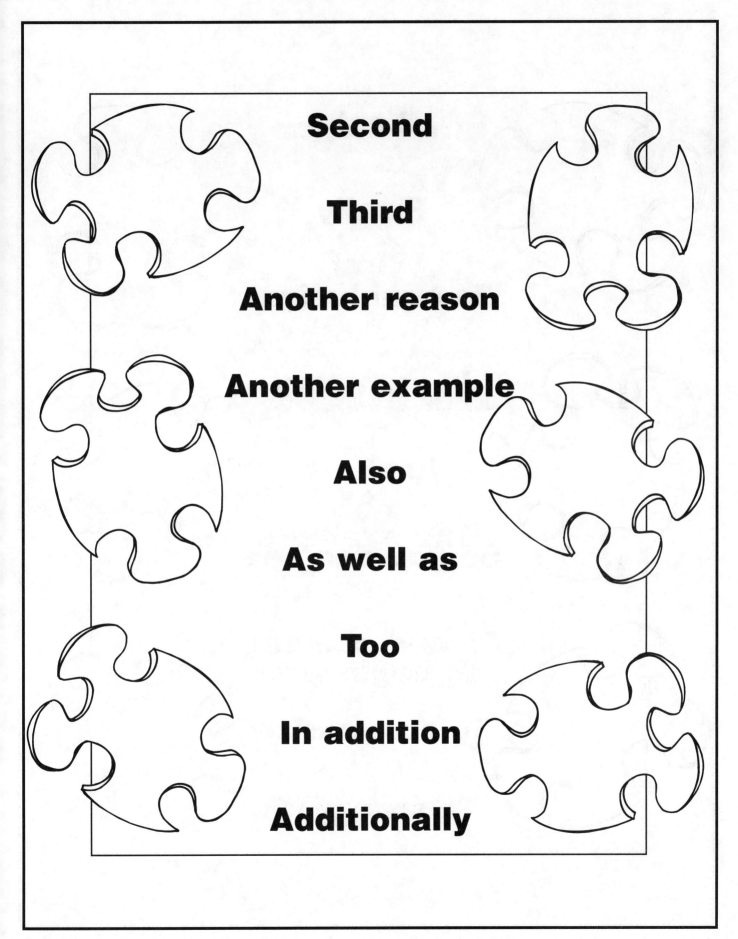

Second

Third

Another reason

Another example

Also

As well as

Too

In addition

Additionally

Color the border of this poster yellow.

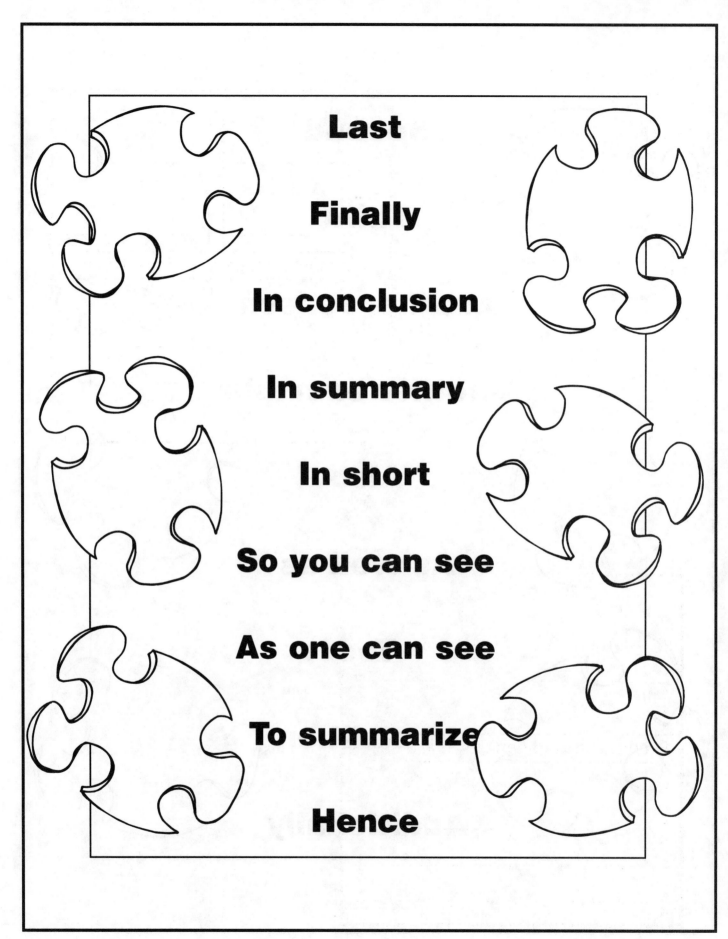

Last

Finally

In conclusion

In summary

In short

So you can see

As one can see

To summarize

Hence

Color the border of this poster red.

Name _____

Directions: Write a reason,
example or explanation in each
box to support the main idea
sentence in the center box.
Give three details for each.
Then choose connecting words.

Puzzle Piece

- _____
- _____
- _____

Puzzle Piece

- _____
- _____
- _____

Computers are a great invention.

Puzzle Piece

- _____
- _____
- _____

Puzzle Piece

- _____
- _____
- _____

Puzzle Piece

- _____
- _____
- _____

Puzzle Piece

- _____
- _____
- _____

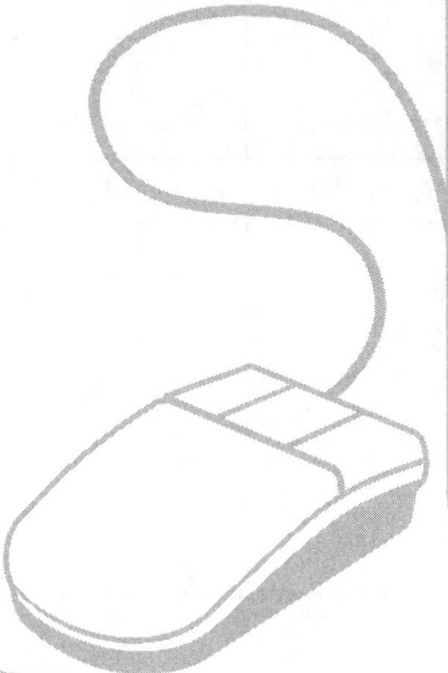

Everyone should participate in a sport.

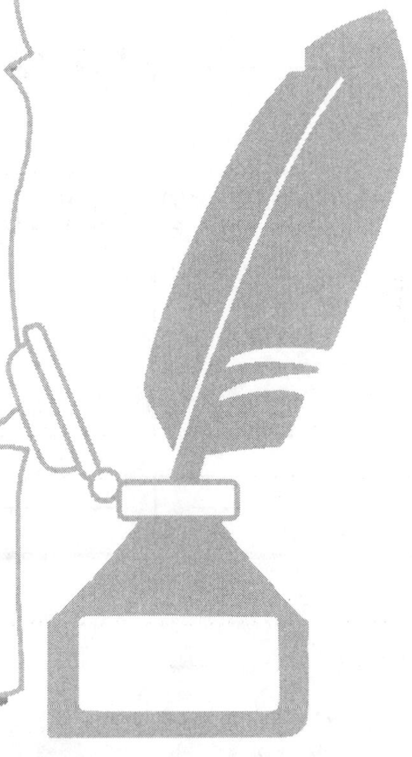

Puzzle Piece

- _____
- _____
- _____

Puzzle Piece

- _____
- _____
- _____

Name _____

Directions: Write a reason, example or explanation in each box to support the main idea sentence in the center box. Give three details for each. Then choose connecting words.

Puzzle Piece

- _____
- _____
- _____

Puzzle Piece

- _____
- _____
- _____

My home state is the best in the U.S.

Puzzle Piece

- _____
- _____
- _____

Puzzle Piece

_____
_____
_____

Puzzle Piece

- _____
- _____
- _____

Puzzle Piece

- _____
- _____
- _____

Just say no to drugs.

Puzzle Piece

- _____
- _____
- _____

Puzzle Piece

_____
_____
_____

Step 4

$$4\square + 3 + C + V$$

Incorporating Vivid Language into Writing

Thus far instruction on the four square organizer has had the goal of building focus, organization and supporting detail into students' writing. This fourth step of instruction begins to assist the writer in developing a style and to use writing as a craft.

Writing with vivid language is achieved by careful, specific word choice. Sensory experiences are an excellent means of providing a vivid expression of thought. Vivid language in writing lets us know what the writer sees, hears, feels, smells and tastes. Vivid language is also heavily involved with the emotional state of the writer.

To explain the need for vivid language, students can be drawn to a favorite medium—television. If you want to explain everything that happened on a particular program that night, you can say there was a "really cool car chase" on a favorite detective show. Or you can say, "There was a detective show where this guy was chasing a '97 red Camaro at high speed up and down the hills of San Francisco. They went squealing past rows of tall, brown apartment buildings. The police car screeched around a corner and whacked into a mailbox. Then the police slammed into a trolley car and, boom, it went up into flames. Meanwhile the bad guys zipped across the Golden Gate until they lost control of their Camaro. The tires were screaming. Then they went silently over the edge until their demise in a tiny splash in the gleaming blue waters below." Ask students in which interpretation is the more vivid description? In which can you picture the action?

To encourage the use of vivid language, students need to be probed. When applying a vivid word to a particular detail, you need to ask students some questions. For instance, if your detail states "a pepperoni pizza," ask students: How does the pizza look? How does it taste? What do you hear? How does it feel? How does it smell? What are your emotions at the particular moment you encounter the pizza? The answers to these questions clarify the composition for the potential reader by giving us more of the picture that the writer "sees" in the mind's eye.

Vivid language writing is not developed overnight, but there are certain techniques that can be employed to encourage its growth. Students can build "Like What?" lists. For instance, a certain attribute may be overused and not provide a vivid enough picture for the reader. The "Like What?" list can be used to give alternate word choices for the writer. It is also an easy way to get students to include a literary device—simile or metaphor.

The "Like What?" exercise can be used to produce some ready references to help writers avoid using jaded language to describe objects or events. Students can generate lists from brainstorming or thesaurus use and post them in a word wall reference area for writers.

You may need to remind students not to get **carried away** with this. They could develop "like" fever!

Cold	Good	Blue
ice	gold	the ocean
Alaska	whipped cream on hot cocoa	the sky
Grandma's hands	air conditioning in the summer	an angel's eyes
a soda can		a blueberry

88

A "Like What?" reproducible is on page 91 so that you can start producing those lists.

On page 90 is a vivid words poster which reminds student writers to engage their five-senses-plus-one when providing vivid language.

Addition of vivids enhances the maturity of writing. This further level of elaboration, usually on a sensory level, helps the writer develop voice. Building these descriptions prepares the young writer for longer compositions.

Continue to read aloud all examples as they are completed. This will facilitate the change over to composition.

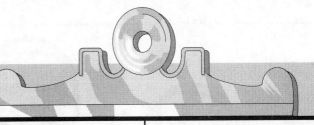

To begin with Recycle	Also Clean up neighborhoods
• **newspapers** in a bundle • **glass** makes new glass • **plastic containers and bottles** melted down	• **pick up trash** laying around • **use wastebasket** set an example • **never litter** if everyone dropped one piece of trash . . .

Everyone can help to save the planet.

Additionally Save water	In conclusion Everyone can help save the planet be recycling, cleaning up our neighborhoods and saving water.
• **on the lawn** don't water too often • **when brushing teeth** shut it off • **Showers not baths** saves gallons	

TRASH

The oral reading of our essay at this stage (Remember, students are writing *only in four square form* this far.):

Everyone can help to save the planet.

If we all recycle there will be much less trash around. Bundle your newspapers and they can be easily recycled. Glass is as good as new when it is recycled because it is made into new glass. When plastic is recycled it is melted down, cleaned up and used again.

Everyone can help clean up his or her own neighborhood. If you see trash laying around, pick it up. Use a wastebasket and set a good example for others. Make sure that you never litter. If every person dropped just one piece of litter on the ground, imagine how much trash there would be around!

Save some water to help Earth. Don't use so much water on the lawn, more than three times a week may be too often. Shut off the faucet when you brush your teeth. Showers use many gallons less water than baths, so why not switch?

Everyone can help save the planet by recycling, cleaning up our neighborhoods and saving water.

Pages 90-93 are wall posters and workbook pages for this step.

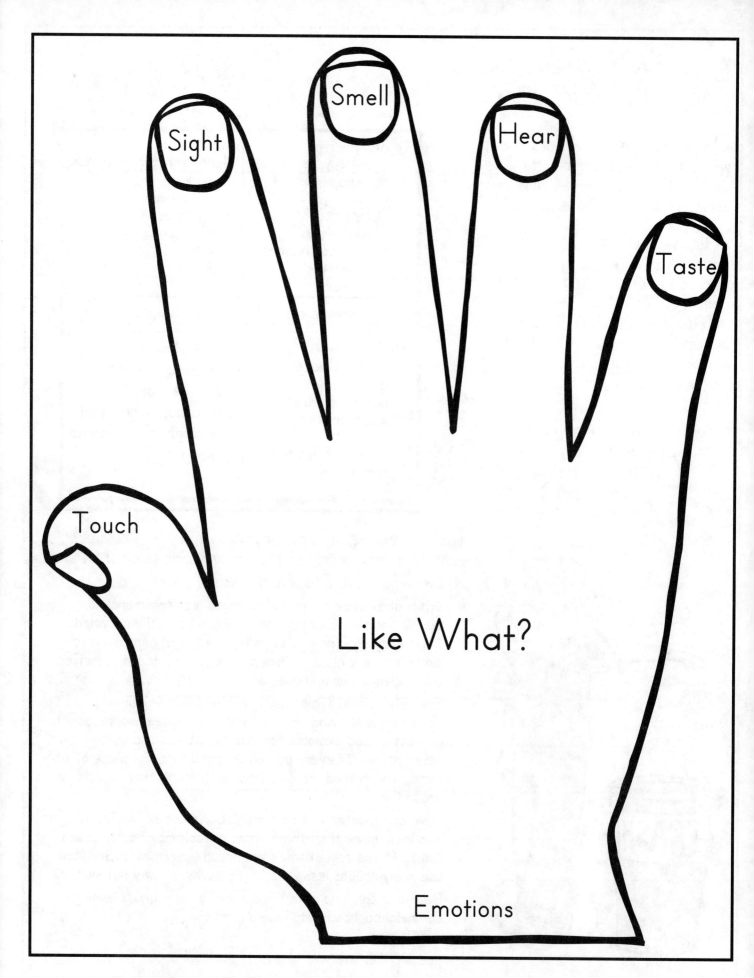

Vivid Words Poster

Like What?

Name _____

Directions: Write a reason, example or explanation in each box to support the main idea sentence in the center box. Give three details for each. Then choose connecting words. Supply one vivid for each detail and circle it.

Puzzle Piece
- _____
- _____
- _____

Puzzle Piece
- _____
- _____
- _____

Our country has a fascinating history.

Puzzle Piece
- _____
- _____
- _____

Puzzle Piece
- _____
- _____
- _____

Puzzle Piece
- _____
- _____
- _____

Puzzle Piece
- _____
- _____
- _____

George Washington was a great man.

Puzzle Piece
- _____
- _____
- _____

Puzzle Piece
- _____
- _____
- _____

Name _____

Directions: Write a reason, example or explanation in each box to support the main idea sentence in the center box. Give three details for each. Then choose connecting words. Supply one vivid for each detail and circle it.

Puzzle Piece
- _____
- _____
- _____

Puzzle Piece
- _____
- _____
- _____

Art class is enjoyable.

Puzzle Piece
- _____
- _____
- _____

Puzzle Piece
- _____
- _____
- _____

Puzzle Piece
- _____
- _____
- _____

Puzzle Piece
- _____
- _____
- _____

You must work hard to be a good student.

Puzzle Piece
- _____
- _____
- _____

Puzzle Piece
- _____
- _____
- _____

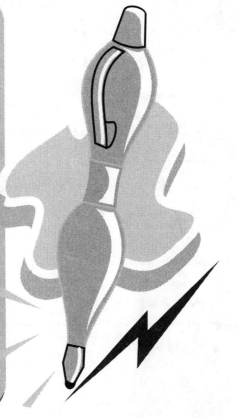

Rote Instruction
4☐ + 3 + C + V = 5 Paragraphs
Taking the Writing off the Organizer

Students have now spent a great deal of time working on the organizer, having never completed the composition phase of the writing process. The oral "story readings" performed with the completed four squares at early stages should have led to the understanding that this was a part of a bigger scheme.

When introducing the concept of moving the information from the four square to the multiple-paragraph essay, it is generally recommended to do a rote lesson. The whole class or group can build a four square together. Then the story is built one sentence at a time. Use chart paper or an overhead transparency with a simulated piece of notebook paper.

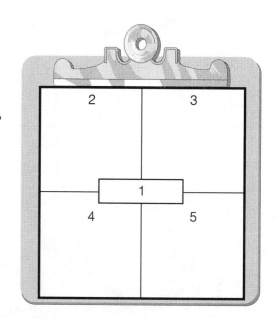

The school week should be shortened to three days. There is a clear need for relaxation and family bonding. Also, this would cause less use of school buses. The evidence supporting this change is clear.

As the composition is being modeled one sentence at a time, students copy it. This "down time" can be used for instant remediation and reminders of the rules of writing in paragraphs. The beauty of the four square is that each time a new box is encountered, it is time to indent. The difficulty of paragraphing has been handled during prewriting.

The four square has built in a good self-checking mechanism for sentence building. Since each of boxes 2, 3 and 4 had four items in them, students can be reminded to check for four capital letters and four periods in each of the corresponding paragraphs.

Remind students never to take the shortcut of trying to list all items in each box as one long sentence. Not only is this poor writing practice, but it is bound to be a run-on sentence.

On pages 95-98 are exercises where the four square is given, and students need only make the transfer of skill to composition.

Name _____

Directions:
For the given four square, write the information in the five-paragraph format.

To begin with	Also
Plants	**Animals**

• variety
  rare
• poisonous
  dangerous to touch
• important
  medicines
	• reptiles
	  tree frogs
	• insects
	  food for reptiles
	• mammals
	  slow moving sloth

Rain forests are complex places.

Additionally	In conclusion
Weather	Rain forests are complex places because of the plants, animals and weather.

• steamy
  near the equator
• wet
  tremendous rainfall
• waterfalls
  flowing water	

Paragraph 1

_____

_____

_____

_____

_____

Paragraph 2

_____

_____

_____

_____

_____

Paragraph 3

_____

_____

_____

_____

_____

Paragraph 4

_____

_____

_____

_____

_____

Paragraph 5

_____

_____

_____

_____

_____

Did you indent each paragraph (five times)?
Do you have your capitals and periods?
Did you write from margin to margin?
Did you avoid Tarzan sentences?

Name _____

Directions:
For the given
four square,
write the
information in
the five-para-
graph format.

First

Honesty

- truthful
  always
- no cheating
  on tests
- confessing
  mistakes

Second

Pay Taxes

- on time
  before April 15
- with pride
  patriotism
- every year
  for rest of life

A good citizen has many traits.

Too

Follow Laws

- traffic laws
  speed limits
- never steal
  robbery
- never fight
  assault

Hence

A good citizen has
many traits such as
honesty, paying taxes
and following laws.

Paragraph 1

_____
_____
_____
_____
_____
_____

Paragraph 2

_____

_____

_____

_____

Paragraph 3

_____

_____

_____

_____

Paragraph 4

_____

_____

_____

_____

Paragraph 5

_____

_____

_____

_____

Did you indent each paragraph (five times)?
Do you have your capitals and periods?
Did you write from margin to margin?
Did you avoid Tarzan sentences?

Improving the Introduction Paragraph
Writing That Thesis Statement

The introductory paragraph is perhaps the most important paragraph in a composition. It is the first impression made on the reader. Also, the first paragraph makes a promise. Explain to the students that the first paragraph in a composition sets the tone of the composition in much the same way that a topic sentence sets the theme of the paragraph. The first paragraph will be used to promise the topic of discourse, as well as prepare the reader for the details to come.

The beauty of the four square writing method is that nearly all the troubles faced in composition will be addressed in the organization stage of the writing process. Students at the secondary level are often asked to write a thesis statement and paper. In the four square, the students have already prepared this information. By writing the wrap-up sentence in box 5 very early in the learning of the four square, students have already practiced this skill.

The first paragraph can now be expanded beyond the one topic sentence. The topic sentence will start the composition. The wrap-up sentence will follow. For the third sentence, the students should write something reflective, thought provoking or a personal feeling. Using this formula gives readers comfort in reading an essay because they will know the topic, be prepared for coming reasoning and be given a little insight into the author's feeling about the topic.

First Paragraph

1. Topic Sentence
(center of four square)

2. Wrap-Up Sentence
(without connecting word)

3. Personal/Reflective Sentence

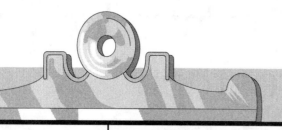

Our "saving the planet" example

To begin with Recycle	Also Clean up neighborhoods
• **newspapers** in a bundle • **glass** makes new glass • **plastic containers and bottles** melted down	• **pick up trash** laying around • **use wastebasket** set an example • **never litter** if everyone dropped one piece of trash . . .

Everyone can help to save the planet.

Additionally Save water	In conclusion
• **on the lawn** don't water too often • **when brushing teeth** shut it off • **Showers not baths** saves gallons	Everyone can help save the planet by recycling, cleaning up our neighborhoods and saving water.

The first paragraph of our "saving the planet" essay:

Everyone can help to save the planet. If we recycle, clean up our neighborhoods, and save water, the planet will be much better off. I am ready to do my part.

Pages 101 and 102 are reproducible worksheet practice pages for the introductory paragraph.

100

Name _____

_____

_____

_____

_____

_____

_____

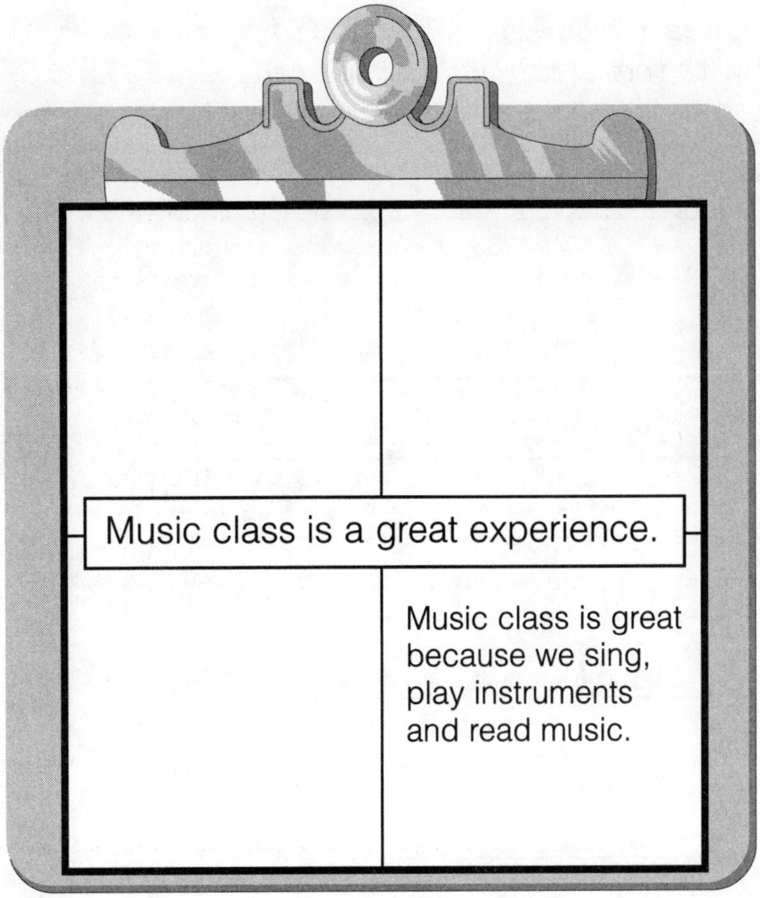

Music class is a great experience.	
	Music class is great because we sing, play instruments and read music.

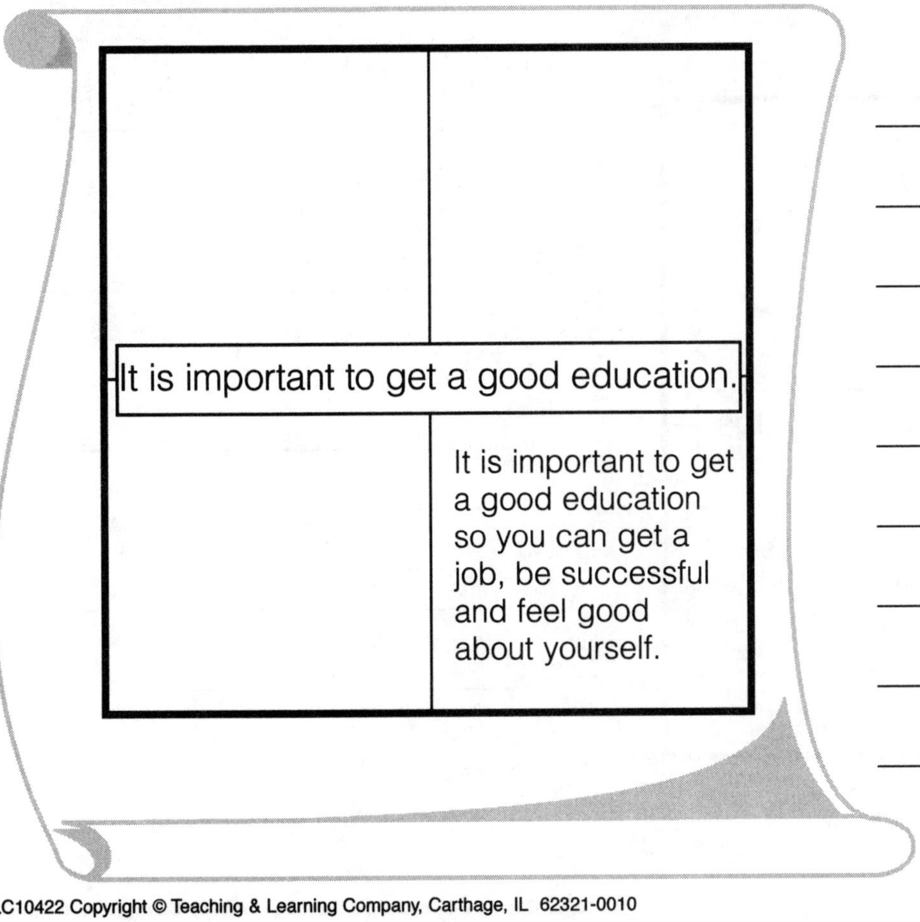

It is important to get a good education.	
	It is important to get a good education so you can get a job, be successful and feel good about yourself.

_____

_____

_____

_____

_____

_____

_____

_____

Name _____

Directions: Write the first paragraph for each four square. Be sure to write topic, wrap-up and personal sentences.

_____

_____

_____

_____

_____

_____

P.E. class is important.	
	P.E. is important because we exercise and learn teamwork and self-discipline.

Kids should stay away from drugs.	
	Stay away from drugs because they are addictive, illegal and can ruin your body.

_____

_____

_____

_____

_____

_____

102

Improving the Final Paragraph
Concluding the Composition

The concluding paragraph in composition carries a great deal of weight. In expository or persuasive writing, this is the writer's final chance to bring home the message to the reader. It is to be used for summary and final emphasis of the main idea.

Using the wrap-up sentence in combination with a "red" connecting word works well in bringing closure to the composition. The recounting of ideas should bring the reader full circle, and the connecting word signifies that this is the composition's end.

At this point of the composition we do not want to add any new information, because it would not be developed. However, after the final wrap-up sentence, it may be appropriate to add a reflective or personal sentence. Encouraging students to end with an exclamatory or interrogative sentence usually gets them thinking. It is also an easy way to get them to add variety to sentence structure.

Final Paragraph

1. Wrap-Up Sentence with Connecting Word

2. Personal/Reflective Sentence, Question or Exclamation

This formula is an easy way to conclude the composition. Encourage students to make that personal sentence perky!

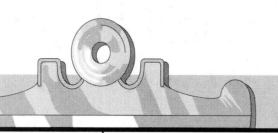

To begin with
    Recycle
- newspapers
  in a bundle
- glass
  makes new glass
- plastic containers
  and bottles
  melted down

Also
Clean up neighborhoods
- pick up trash
  laying around
- use wastebasket
  set an example
- never litter
  if everyone dropped one
  piece of trash . . .

Everyone can help to save the planet.

Additionally
    Save water
- on the lawn
  don't water too often
- when brushing teeth
  shut it off
- Showers not baths
  saves gallons

In conclusion
Everyone can help
save the planet be
recycling, cleaning up
our neighborhoods and
saving water.

The final paragraph of our "save the planet" essay:

In conclusion, everyone can help save the planet by recycling, cleaning up our neighborhoods and saving water. Don't you think this planet is worth saving?

Pages 105 and 106 are reproducible worksheet practice pages for the concluding paragraph.

Directions: Write the final paragraph
for each four square. Be sure to
include the wrap-up and a personal
sentence, question or exclamation.

_____

_____

_____

_____

_____

_____

_____

	A good citizen has many traits.
	A good citizen is honest, tax-paying and law-obeying.

It takes hard work to get all As.	
	To get all A report cards you must study, pay attention and stay organized.

_____

_____

_____

_____

_____

_____

_____

_____

Name _____

Directions: Write the final paragraph for each four square. Be sure to include the wrap-up and a personal sentence, question or exclamation.

_____
_____
_____
_____
_____
_____
_____

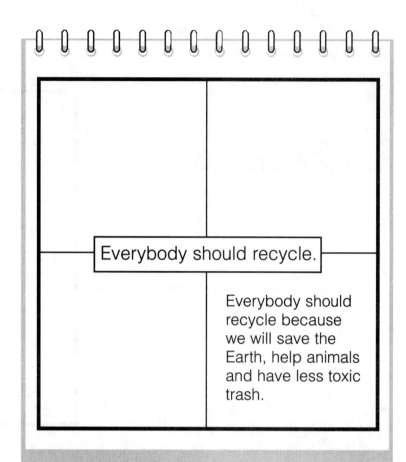

Everybody should recycle.

Everybody should recycle because we will save the Earth, help animals and have less toxic trash.

It is important to have a goal.

It is important to have a goal because it keeps you focused, gives you hope and makes you stronger.

_____
_____
_____
_____
_____
_____
_____
_____

Using the Four Square for Content Area Writing

If you are using the Four Square for writing lessons, it can be simple to use for content applications by using the organizer in its original form, or by varying the function of some of the different boxes. An easy way to assess learning in a content area is to have students write about a topic of study. You may assign the topic in advance, and invite students to complete the Four Square in preparation for the assessment. Using texts, notes and other learning materials students can complete their planner. This asks them to reread, synthesize and make decisions about the information. Sometimes, you may choose to have the students bring the prepared Four Square to the assessment. In this way, you are encouraging the studying and note-taking on the material, and you can easily assess the content.

On the following pages are examples of Four Square templates for some typical styles of academic writing. These may be adapted for other content area writing as well.

When using the Four Square to plan writing, each box becomes a paragraph or section of the paper.

Four Square Book Review

Description of Characters

_____

- Detail _____
- Detail _____
- Detail _____

Brief Synopsis of Plot

- Detail _____
- Detail _____
- Detail _____

Book Title: _____

Author: _____

Publisher: _____

Date of Publication: _____

One of the best parts was . . .

_____

- Detail _____
- Detail _____
- Detail _____

Writer's recommendation for this book. What readers would like it and why.

_____

_____

_____

_____

_____

_____

Four Square Lab Report

Hypothesis

- Why?_____

- Why?_____

- Why?_____

Procedure

- Steps that were followed (in detail)

  _____

- Steps that were followed (in detail)

  _____

- Steps that were followed (in detail)

  _____

Question proposed:

_____
_____

Materials:

_____
_____

Date Collected

- Observations and data

- Observations and data

- Observations and data

What conclusions did you draw and why?

_____

_____

_____

_____

_____

_____

Four Square for a "State" Report

Geography of the State

- Detail _____
- Detail _____
- Detail _____

Main Crops or Natural Resources

- Detail _____
- Detail _____
- Detail _____

State: _____

Symbols: _____

Motto: _____

Population: _____

Region: _____

Businesses or Industries

- Detail _____
- Detail _____
- Detail _____

Places to Visit in the State

- Detail _____
- Detail _____
- Detail _____

Four Square for
Mathematical Story Problems

Decide on the Operation

Which do you choose and why?

Compute

Add, subtract, multiply or divide.

Survey the question.

Key Words: _____

Numbers: _____

What are we looking for? _____

Check your work.

Does your answer make sense?
Check it by doing the opposite operation.

Write to explain what you did and why.

_____

_____

_____

_____

_____

_____

_____

_____

Four Square for Longer Research Topics

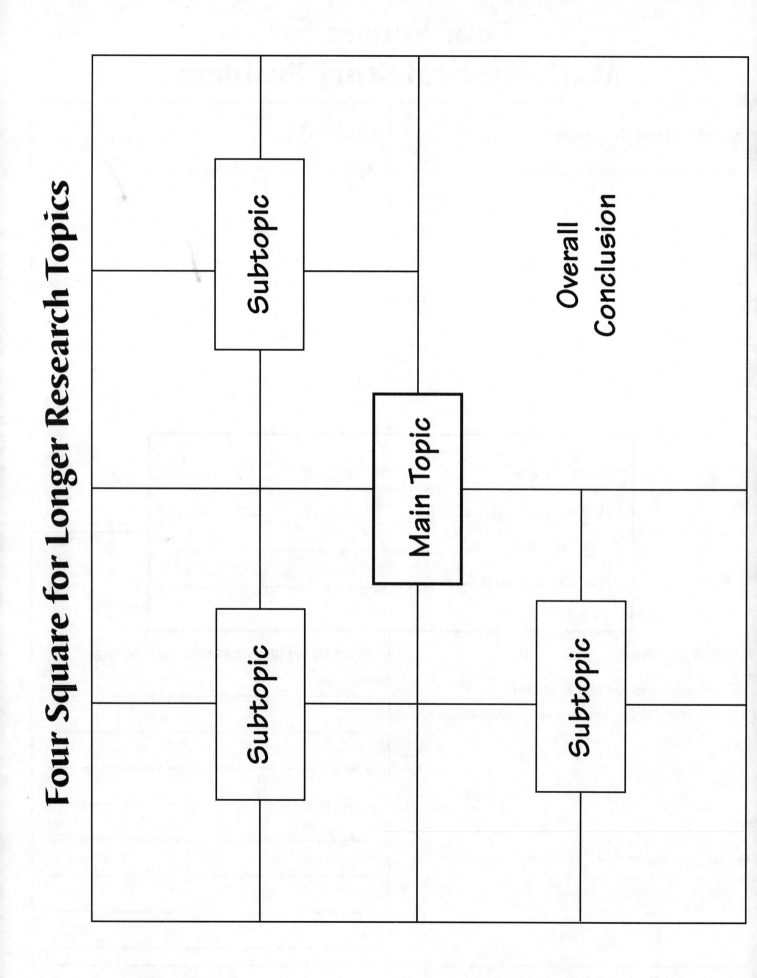

Subtopic

Subtopic

Main Topic

Subtopic

Overall Conclusion

TLC10422 Copyright © Teaching & Learning Company, Carthage, IL 62321-0010